So Many Hats, So Little Hair
A Principal's Tale

by
Char Forsten, Jim Grant, and Betty Hollas

Illustrated by
Patrick Belfiori

Crystal Springs
BOOKS

Published by Crystal Springs Books • Peterborough, New Hampshire
1-800-321-0401

So Many Hats, So Little Hair: A Principal's Tale

by Char Forsten, Jim Grant, and Betty Hollas

Illustrations by Patrick Belfiori
Design by Soosen Dunholter

Published by Crystal Springs Books
75 Jaffrey Road
PO Box 500
Peterborough, NH 03458
Phone: 1-800-321-0401
Fax: 1-800-337-9929
Internet: www.crystalsprings.com

ISBN 1-884548-50-4

Dedication

We dedicate this book to Dick Dunning—principal, teacher, community member, Vietnam veteran, husband, father, and friend—who has donned at least as many hats as are represented in this tale. With thanks to men and women who, like Dick, unselfishly wear each hat with pride and dedication. You make a difference.

A Cautionary Tale

Heather and Josh, two friends both earning teaching degrees, were debating whether to take courses geared toward school administration, as they thought they might like to eventually become principals. Before either made a decision, though, they wanted to discuss the matter further with someone in the field.

As luck would have it, while attending a conference early that autumn, they bumped into Heather's former elementary school principal, Mrs. Allen, who Heather knew would most certainly be able to impart time-tested words of wisdom. But Mrs. Allen was one of the conference presenters and unfortunately didn't have time to talk; maybe they could all get together later that fall, she suggested, "when things settled down." So they said their good-byes and parted ways.

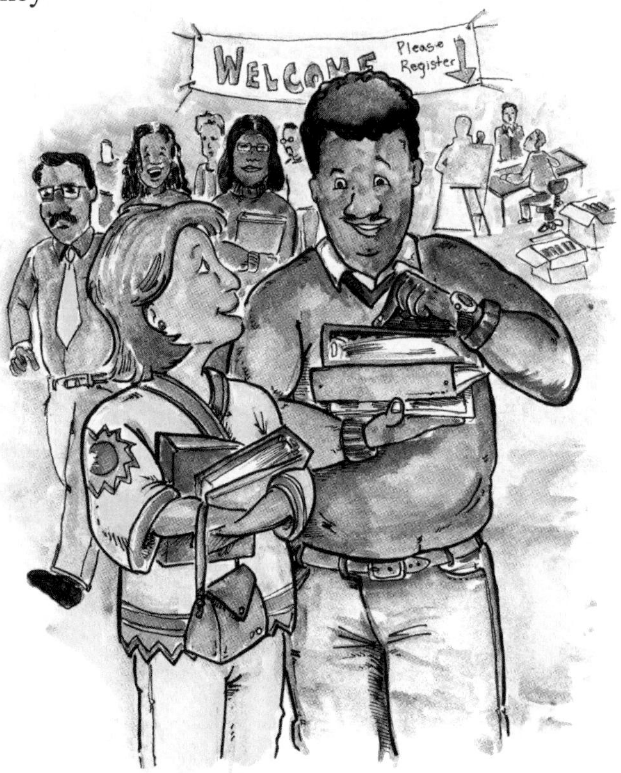
WELCOME
Please Register

"Heather!" Mrs. Allen suddenly called from down the corridor. "So many hats, so little hair!" And with that she smiled, turned, and disappeared into the crowd. Heather and Josh looked quizzically at one another, but figured Mrs. Allen would explain everything when they met later that autumn. As it would happen, however, things never did "settle down," but Heather and Josh graduated that spring, and both did eventually become school principals.

This is their tale.

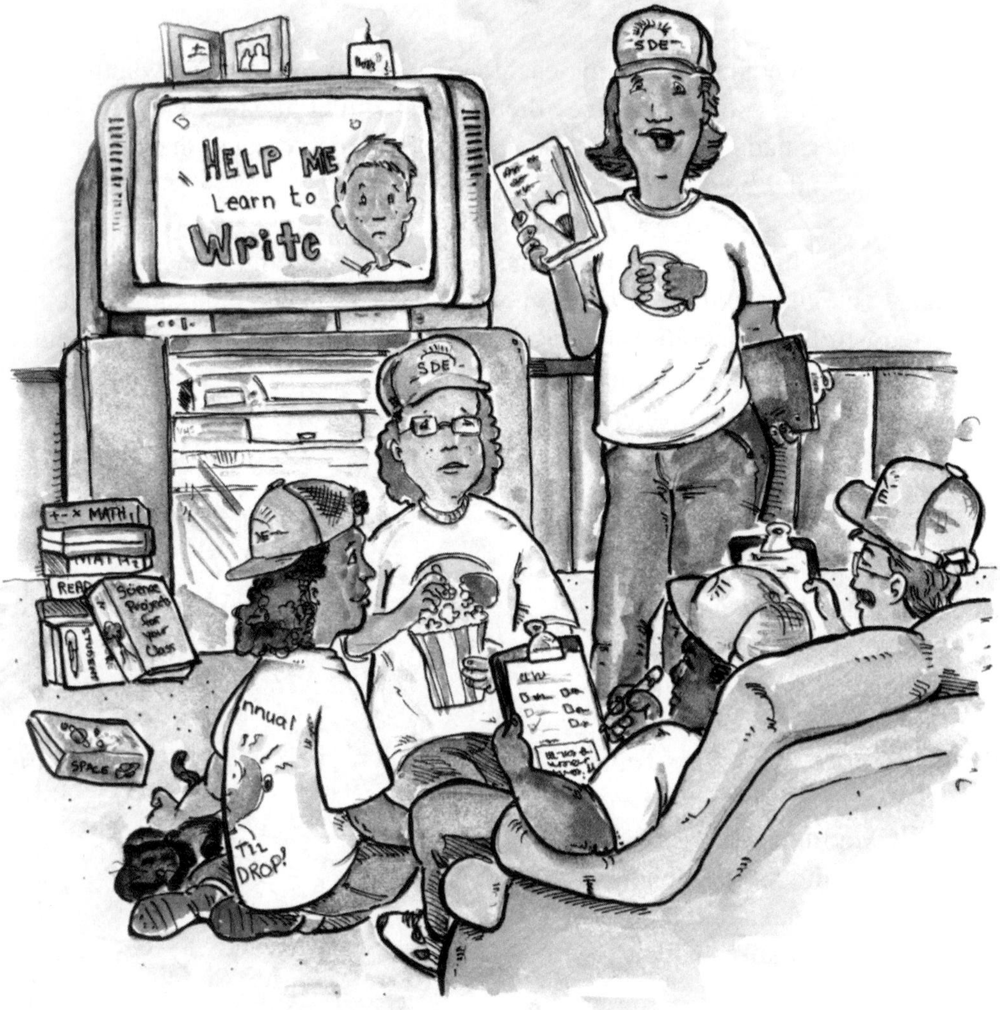
HELP ME
Learn to
Write
SDE
SDE
MATH
READ
Science Projects for Your Class
SPACE
nnual
DROP!

Principals watch movies.

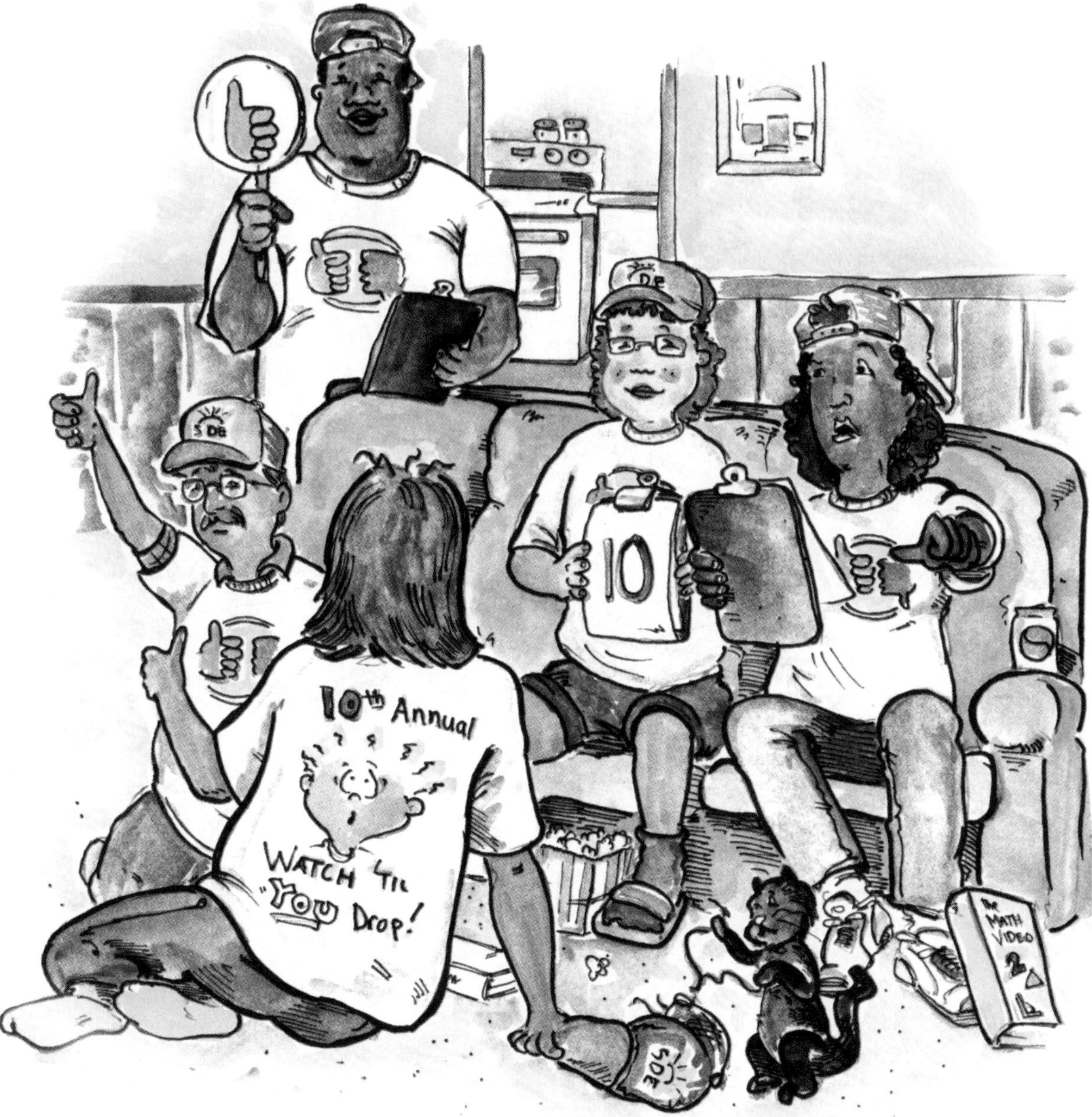

10th Annual
WATCH 'til "YOU" Drop!
10
THE MATH VIDEO 2

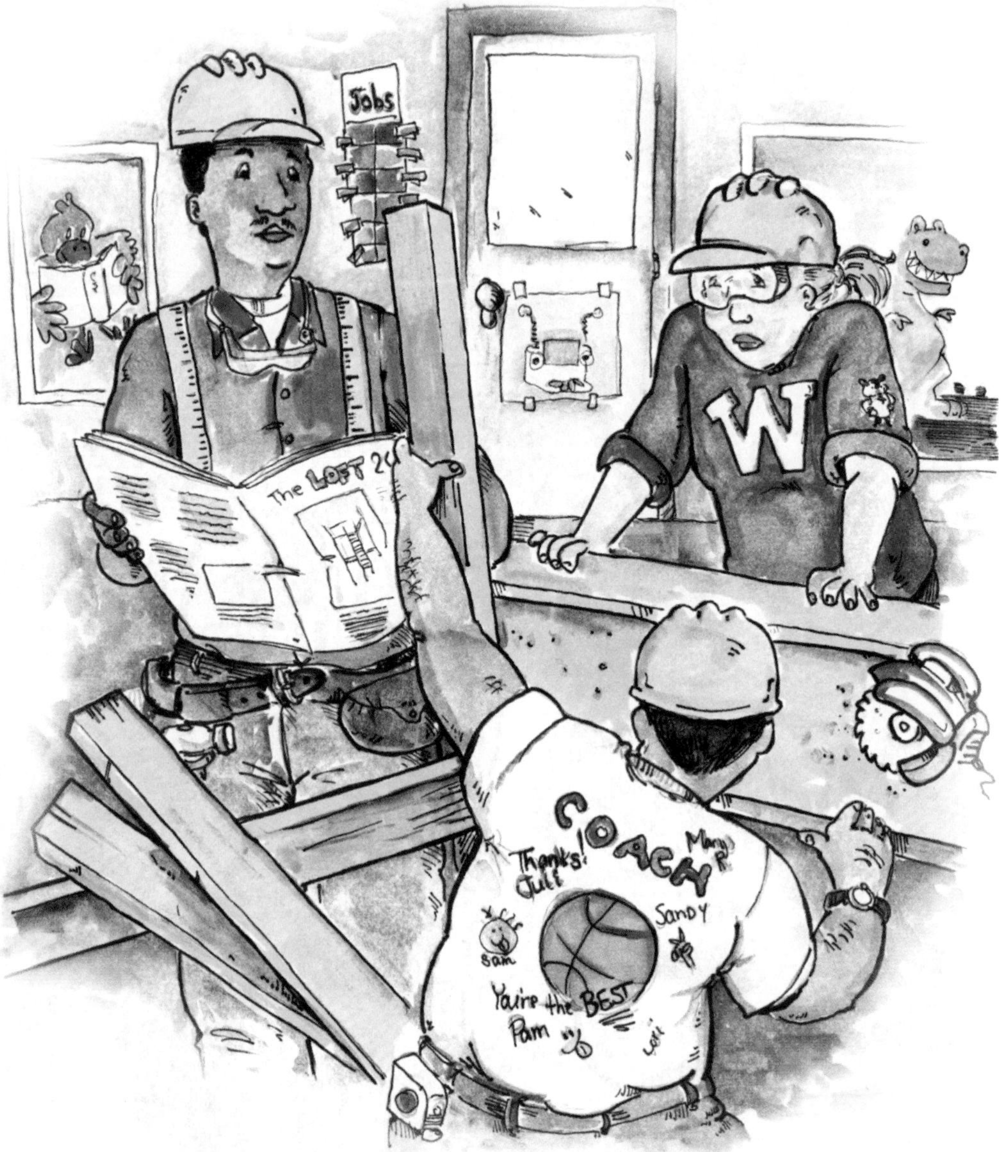
Jobs
COACH
Thanks!
Sandy
You're the BEST
Pam

Principals have lofty ideas.

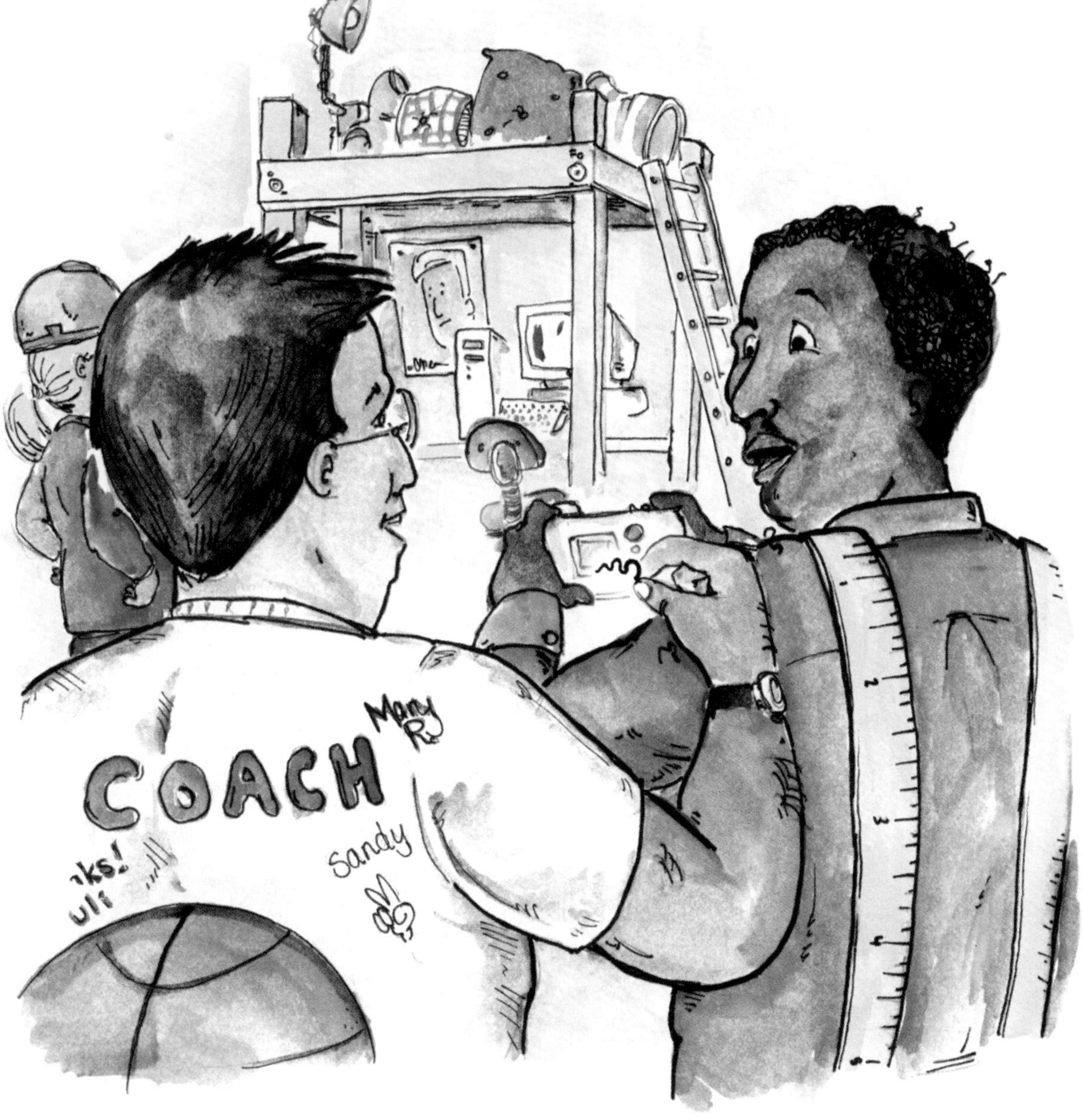
Mary R.
COACH
Sandy

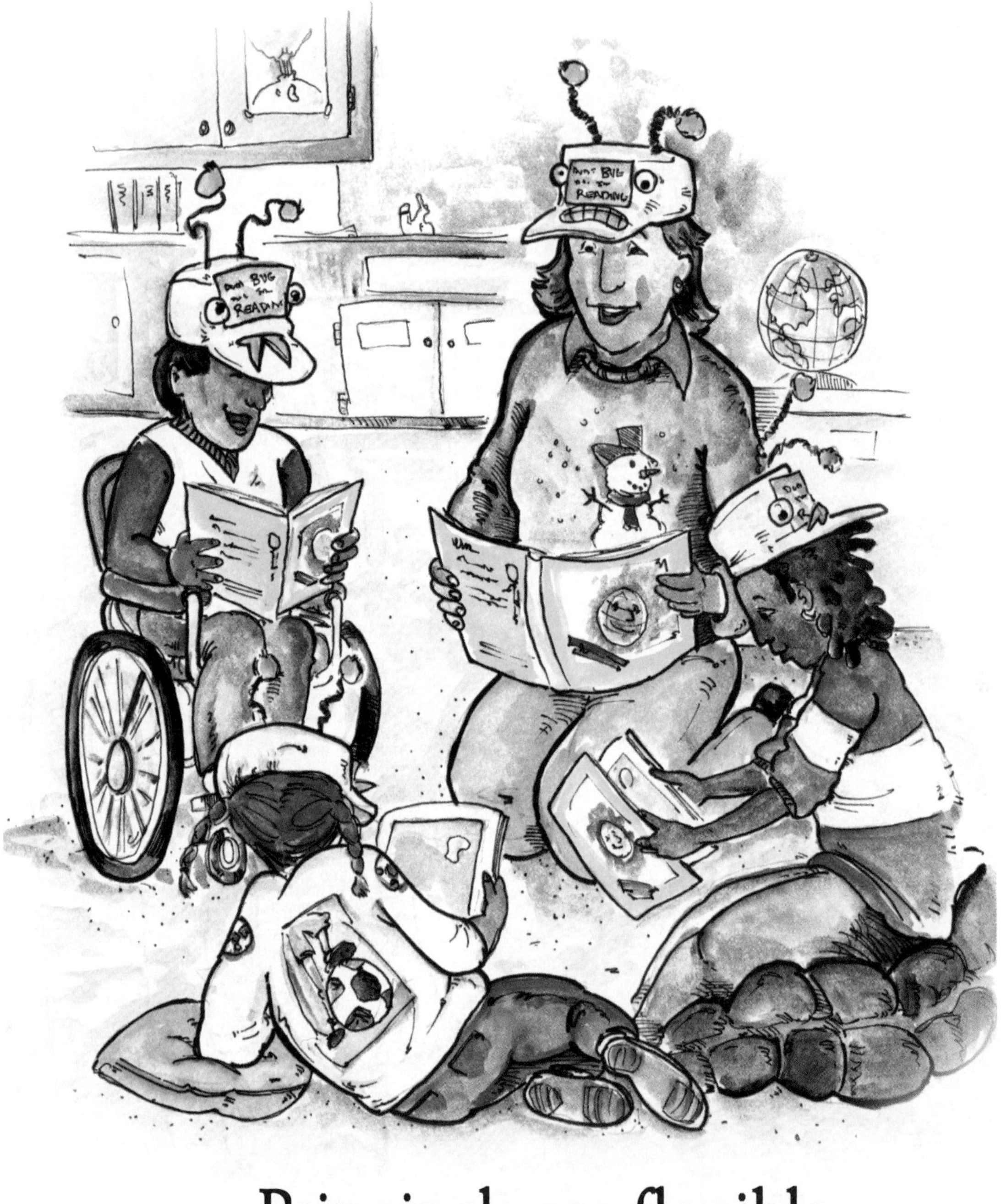
READING

Principals are flexible.

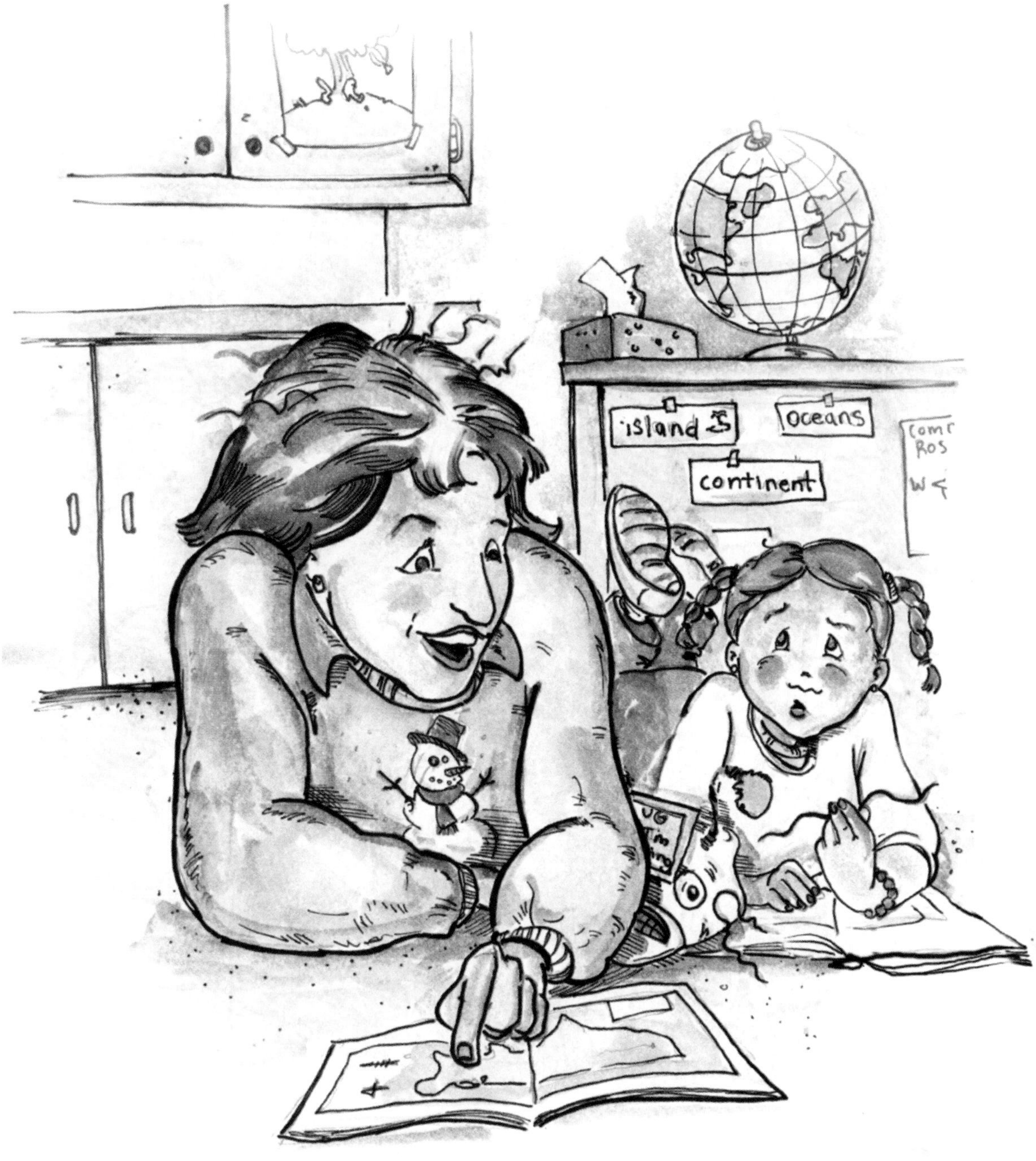
island
oceans
continent

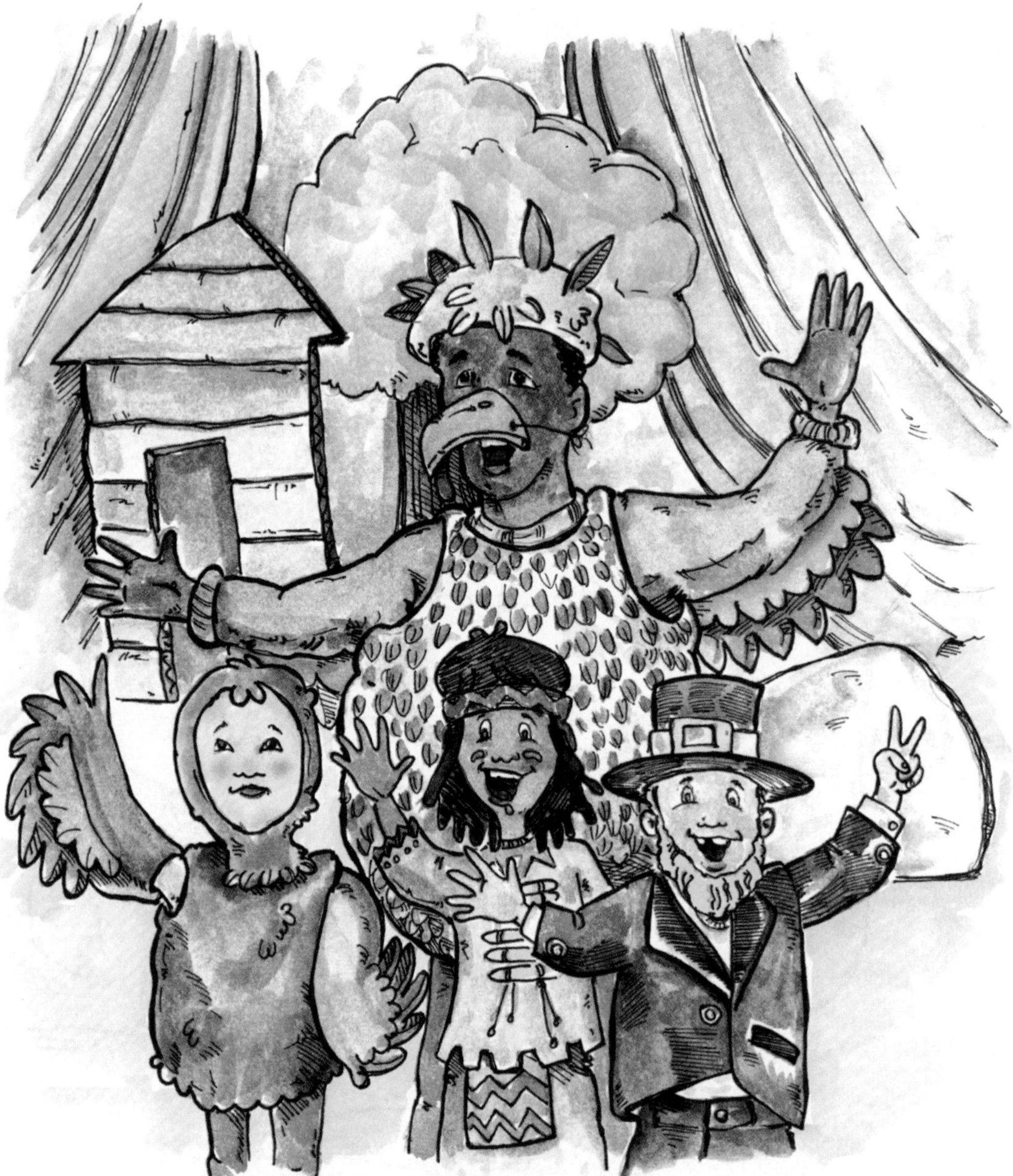

Principals take center stage.

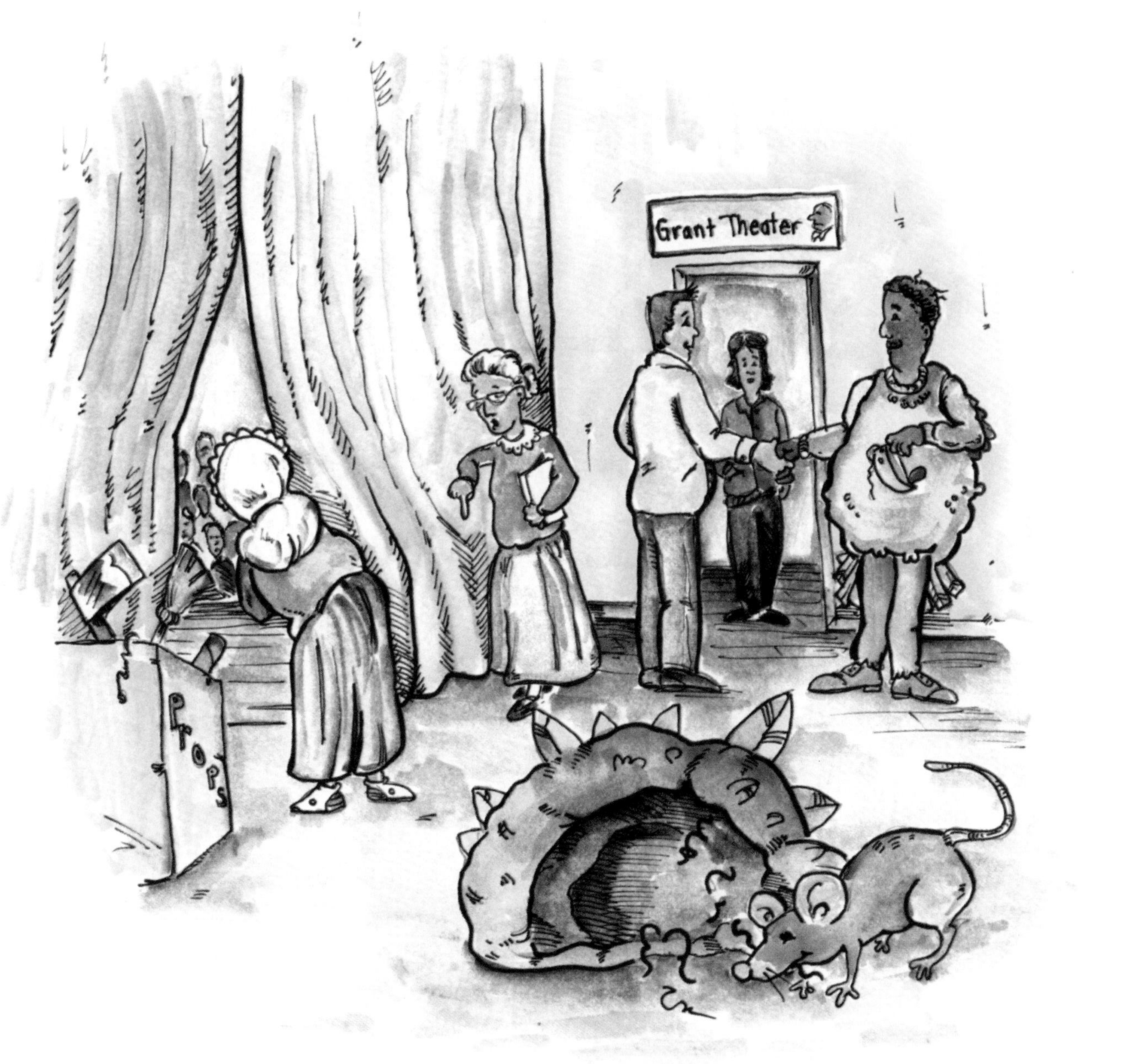
Grant Theater
PROPS

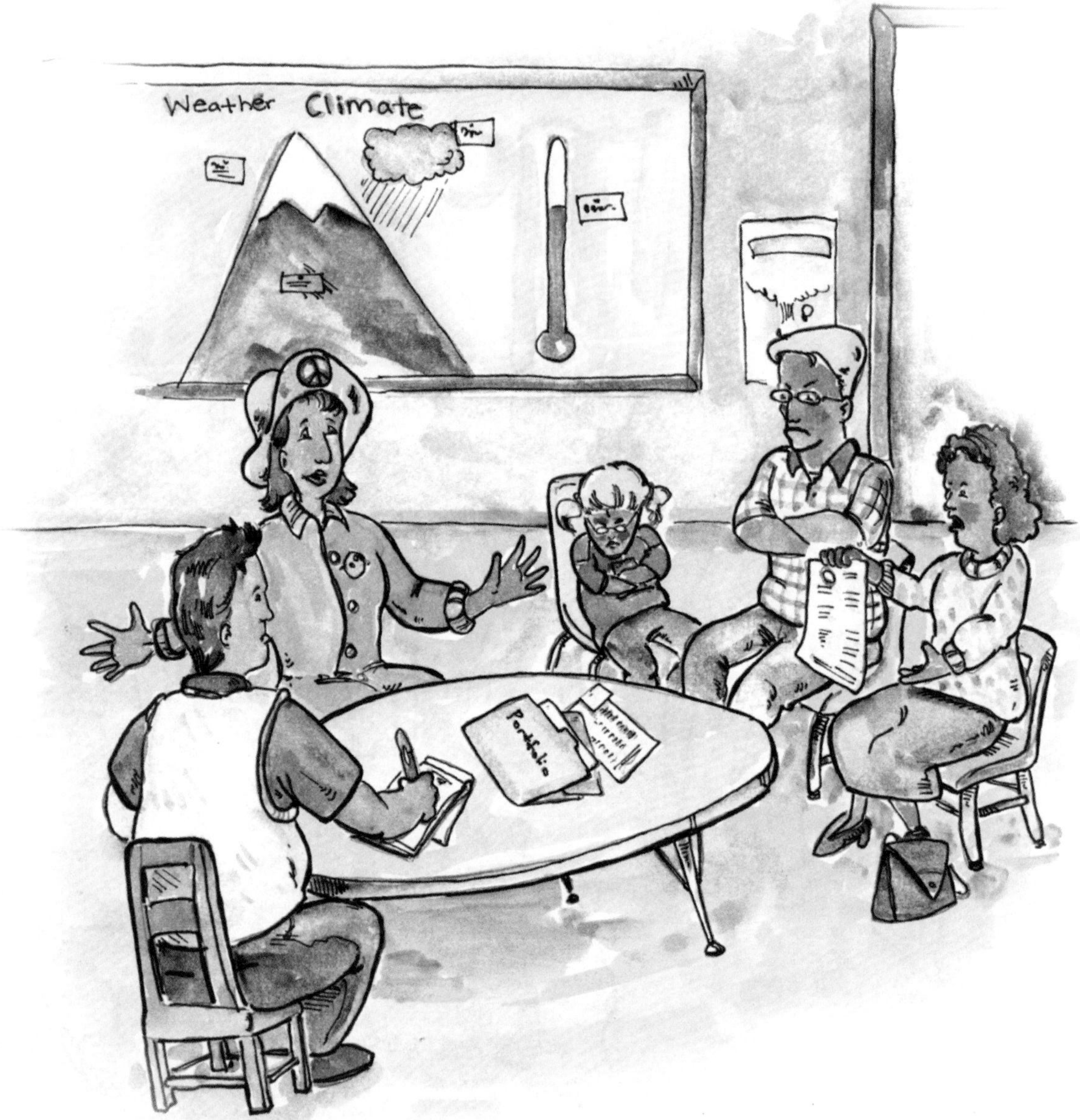
Weather
Climate
Portfolio

Principals negotiate peace deals.

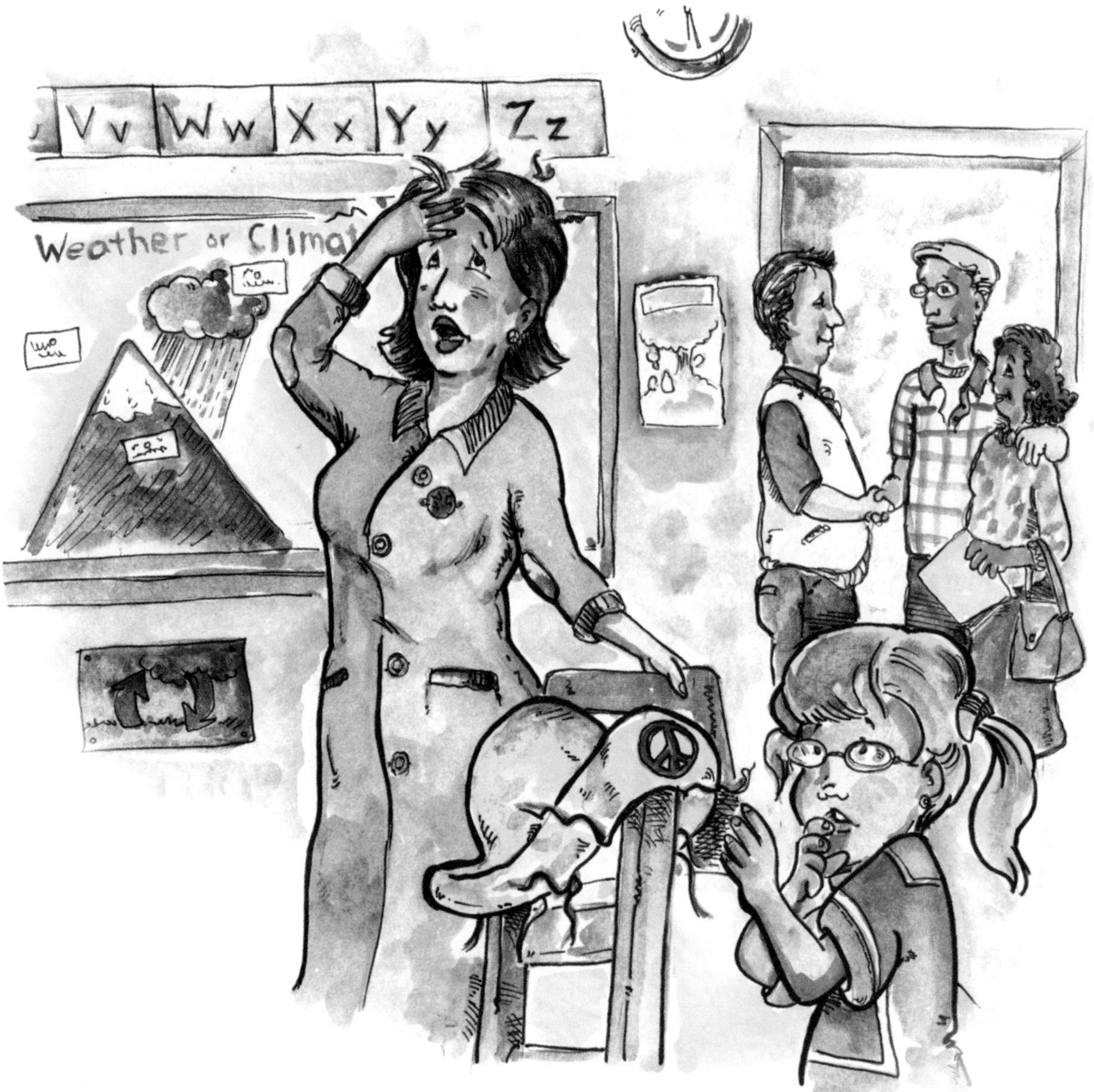

Vv Ww Xx Yy Zz
Weather or Climat

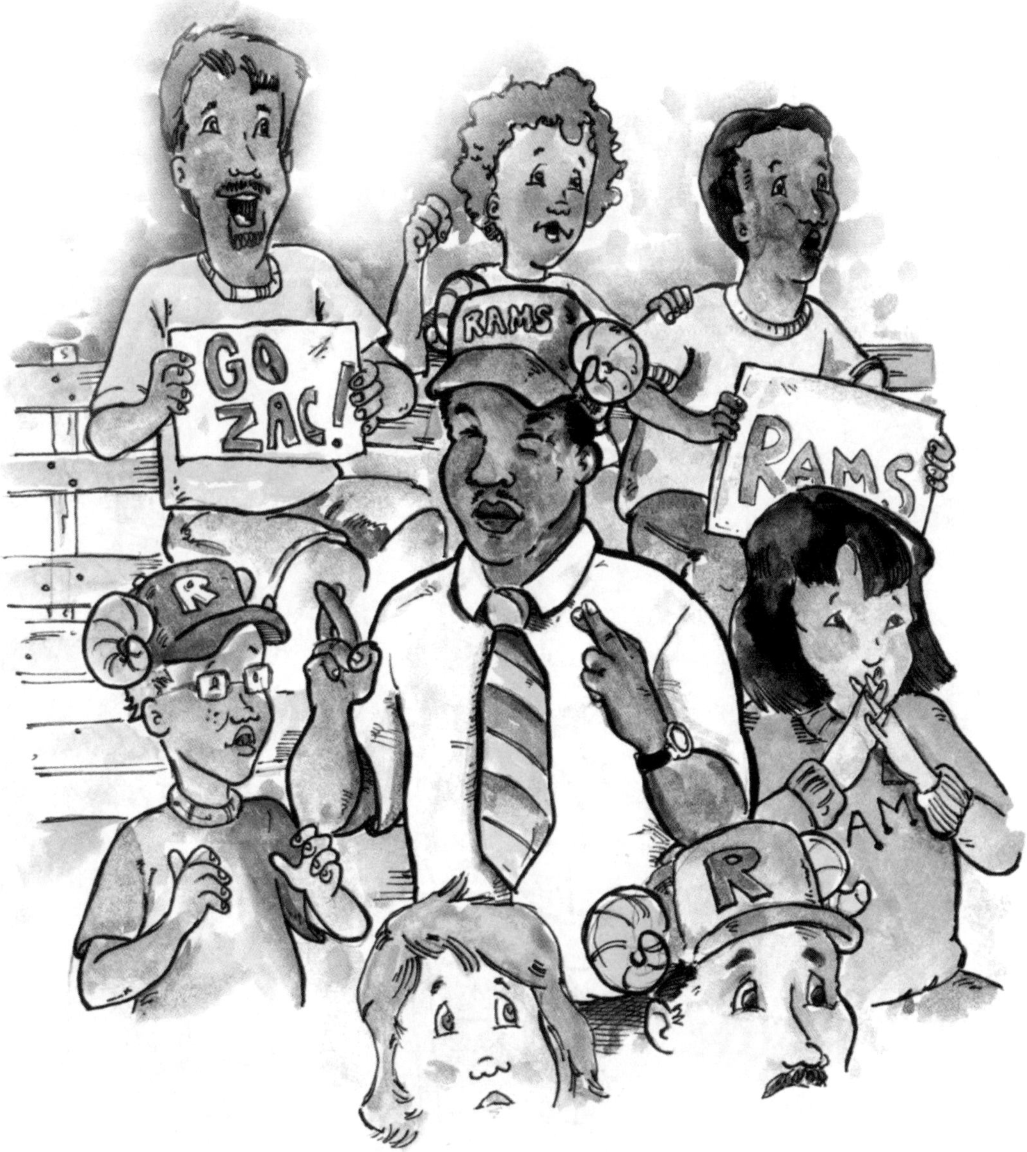

GO ZAC!
RAMS
RAMS
R
R
R
RAM

Principals go out at night.

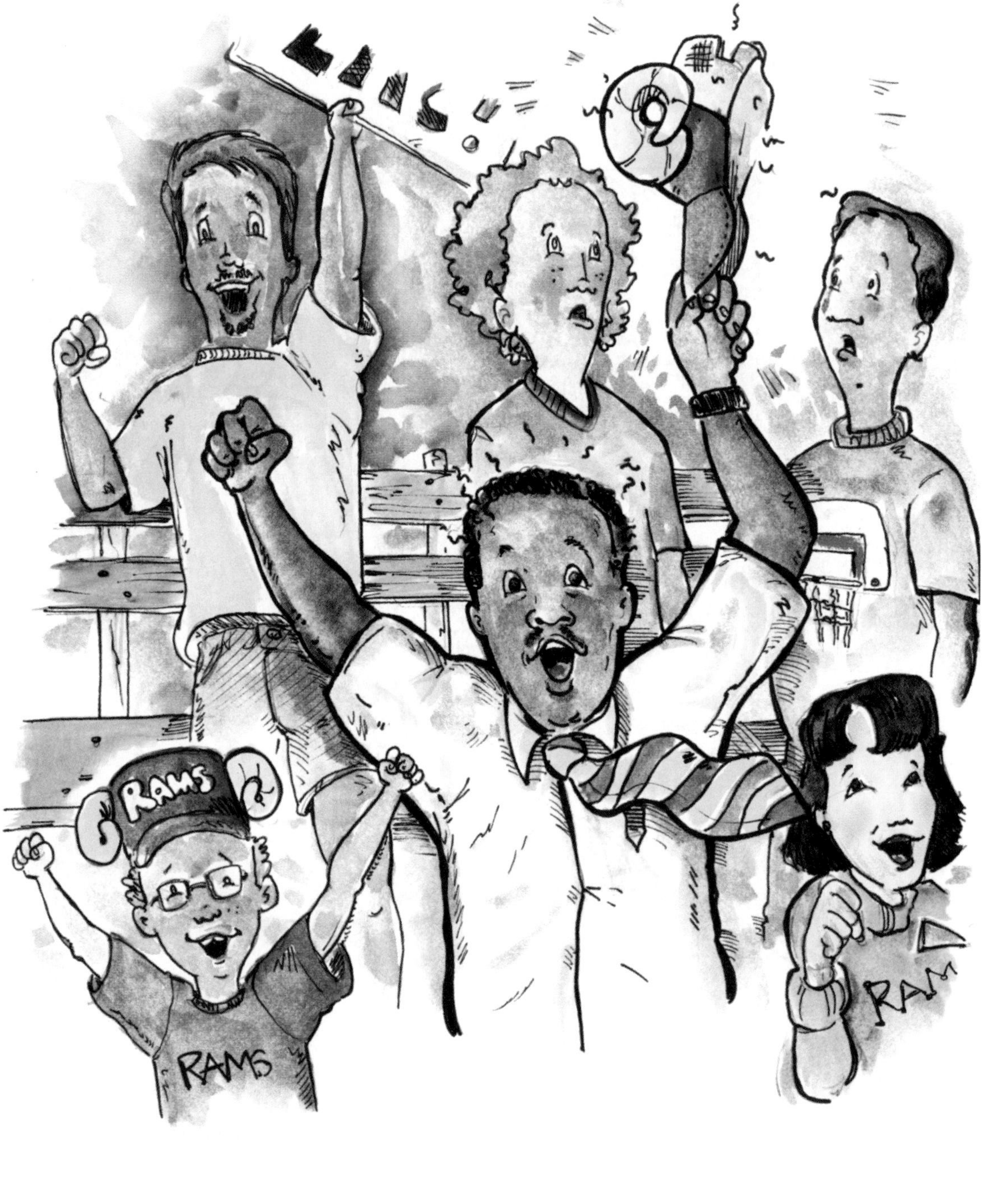
RAMS
RAMS
RAM

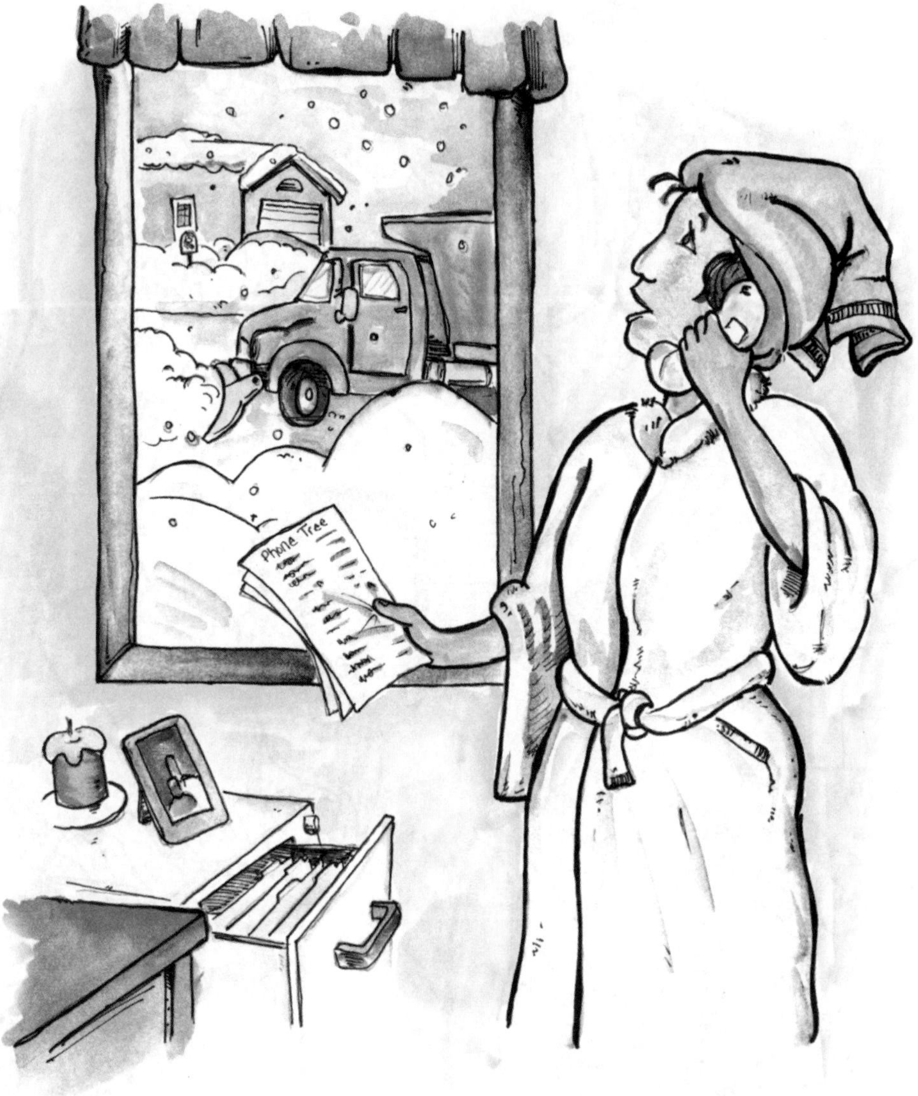
Phone Tree

Principals give weather updates.

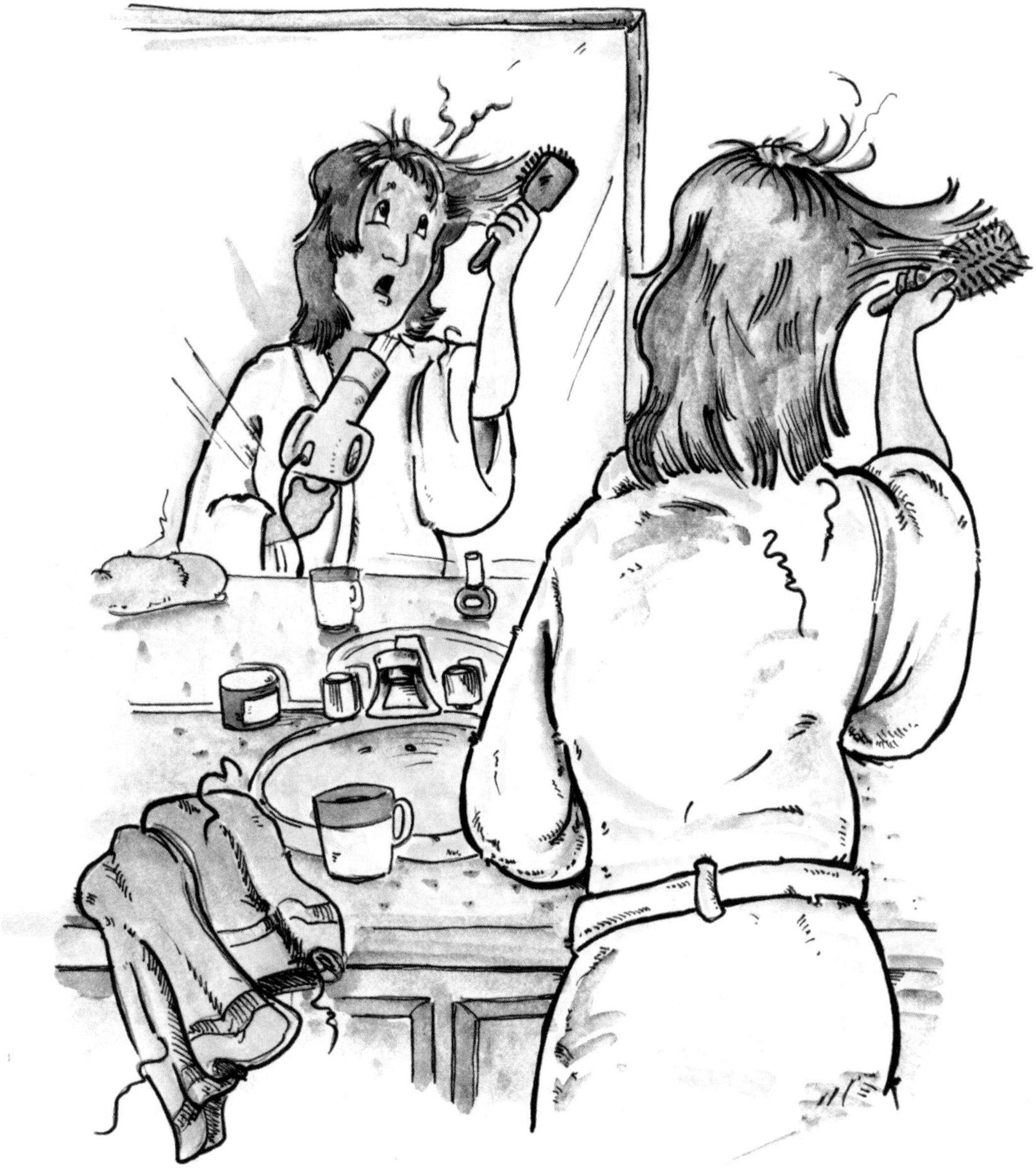

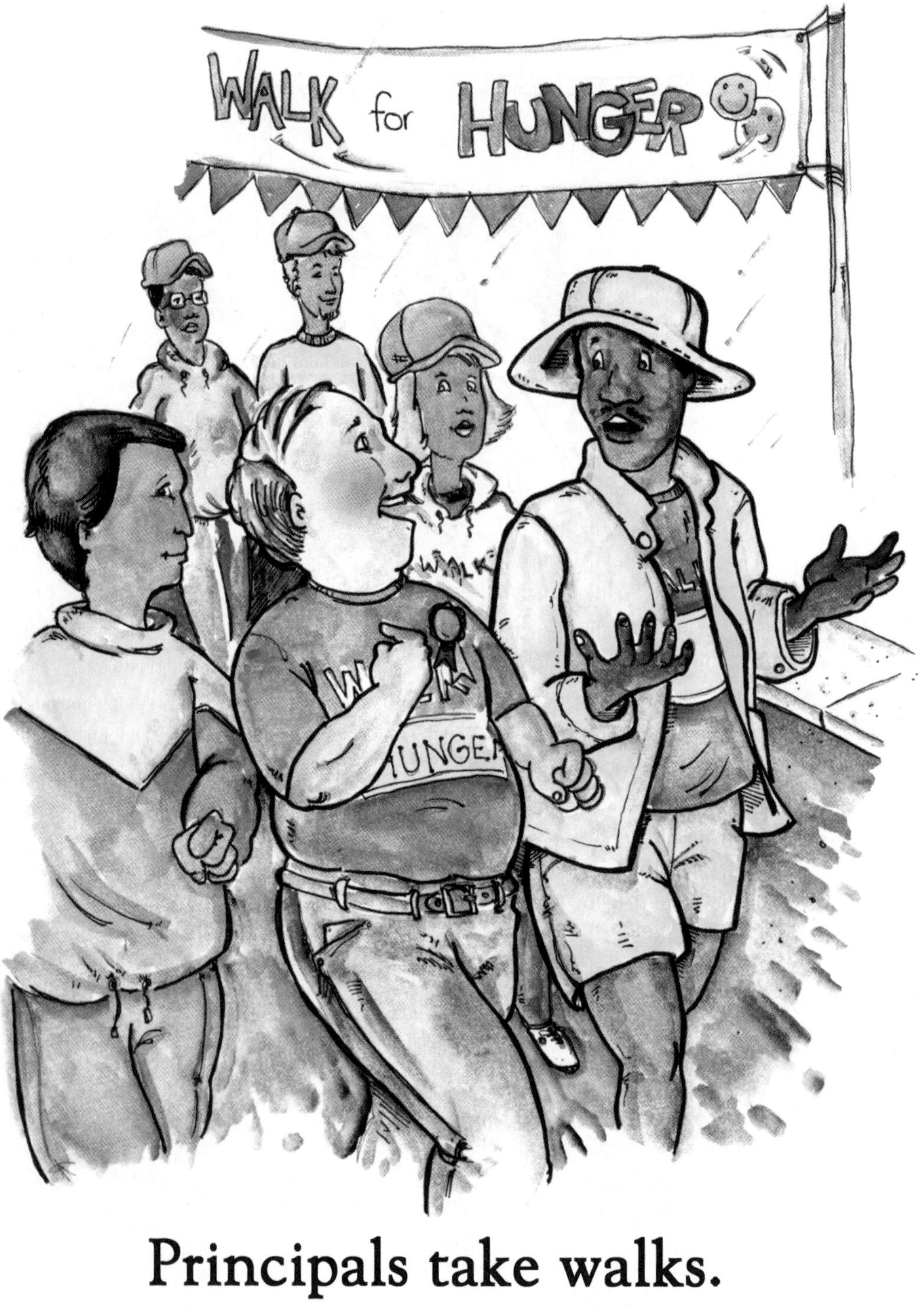
WALK for HUNGER 99
WALK
HUNGER

Principals take walks.

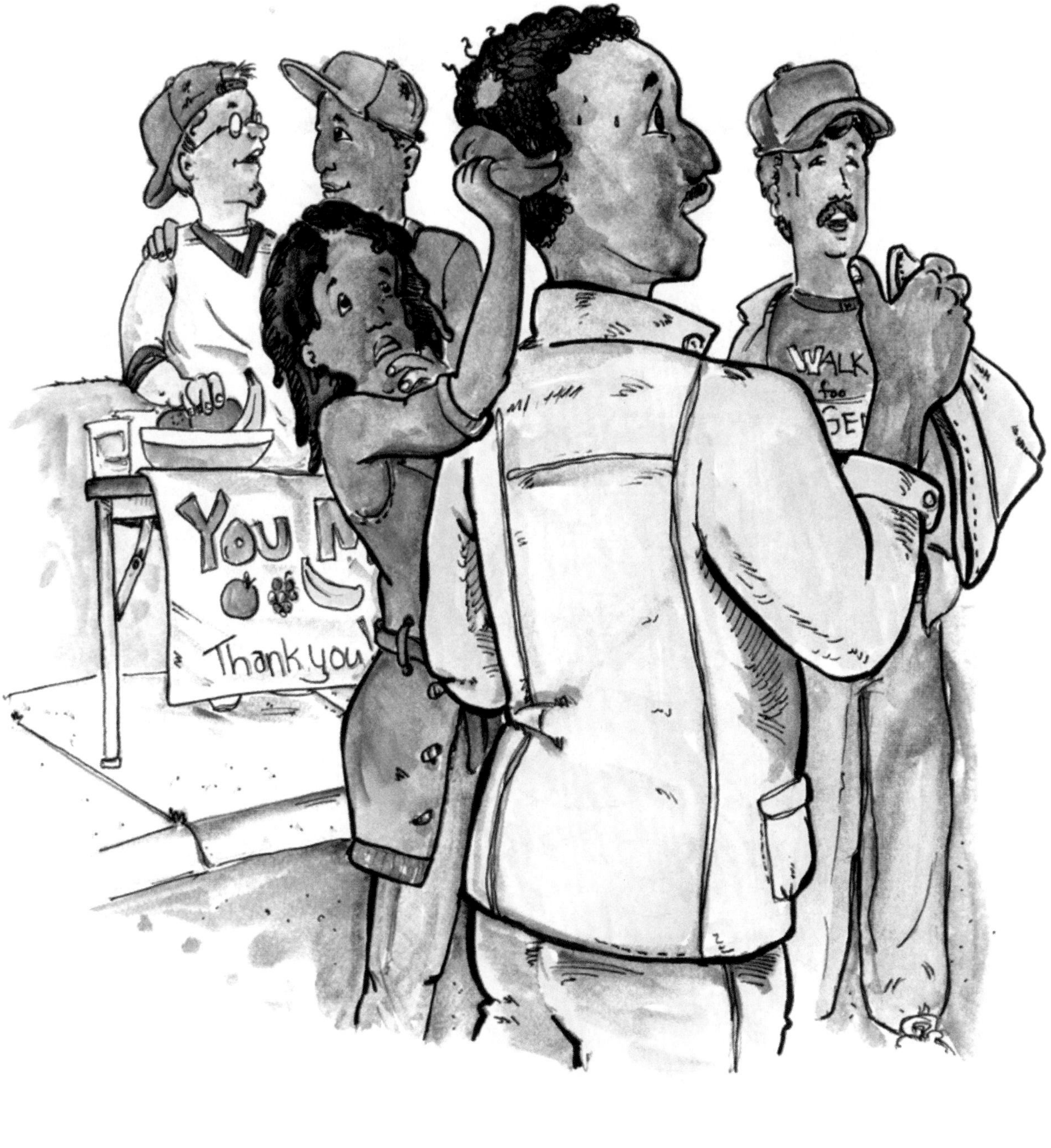
YOU
Thank you!
WALK

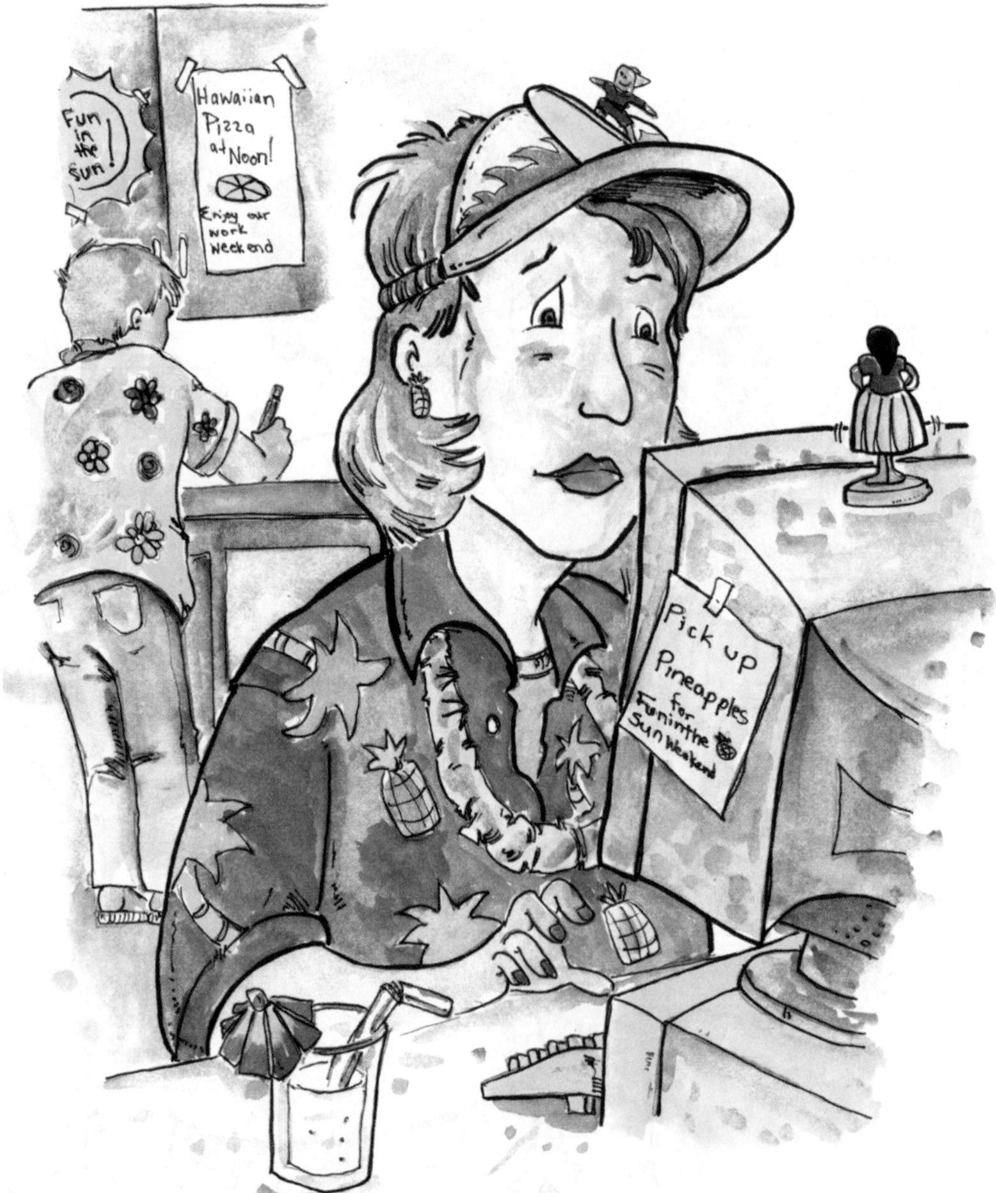
Fun in the Sun!
Hawaiian Pizza at Noon!
Enjoy our work weekend
Pick up Pineapples for Fun in the Sun Weekend

Principals surf.

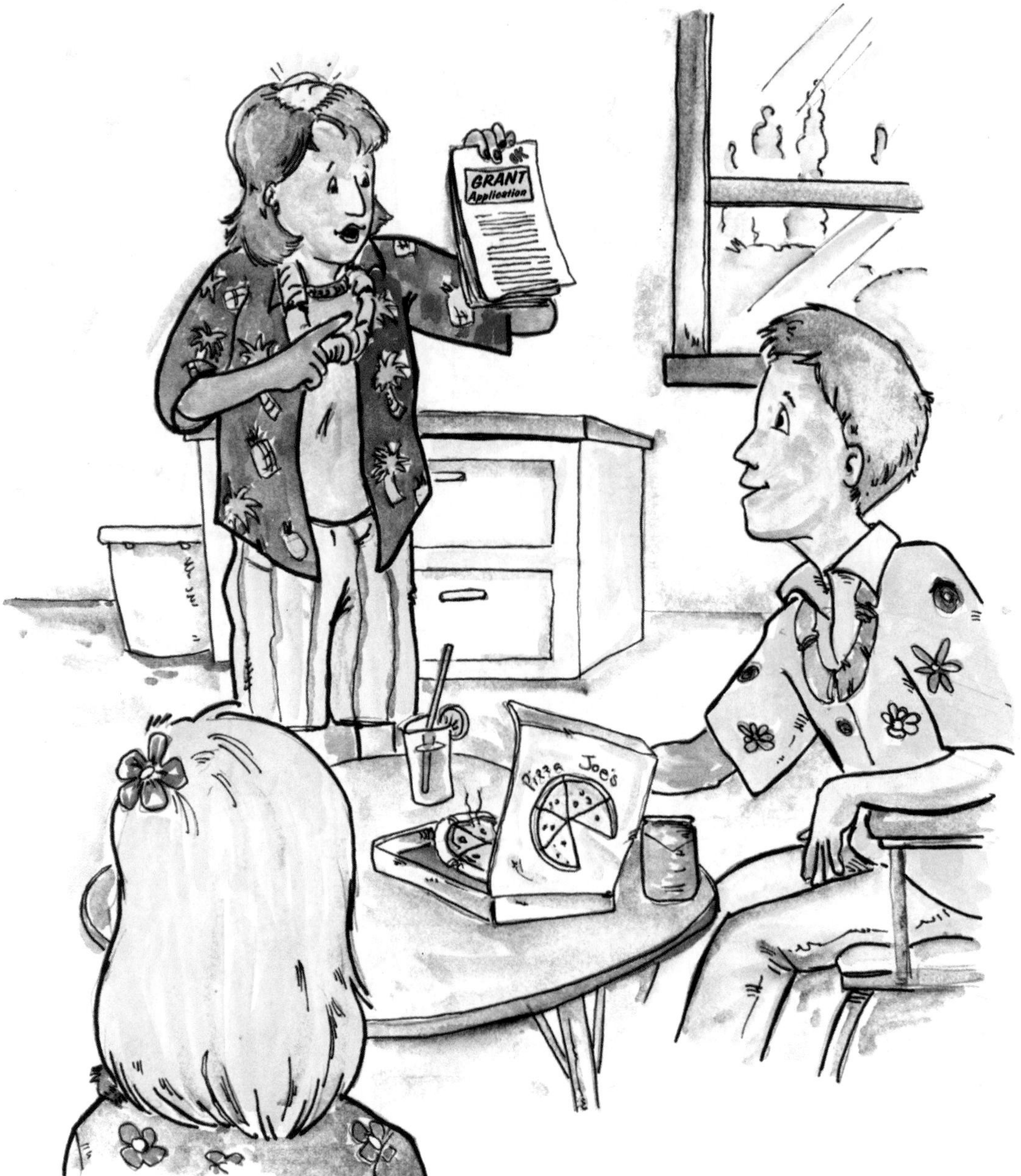
GRANT Application
Pizza Joe's

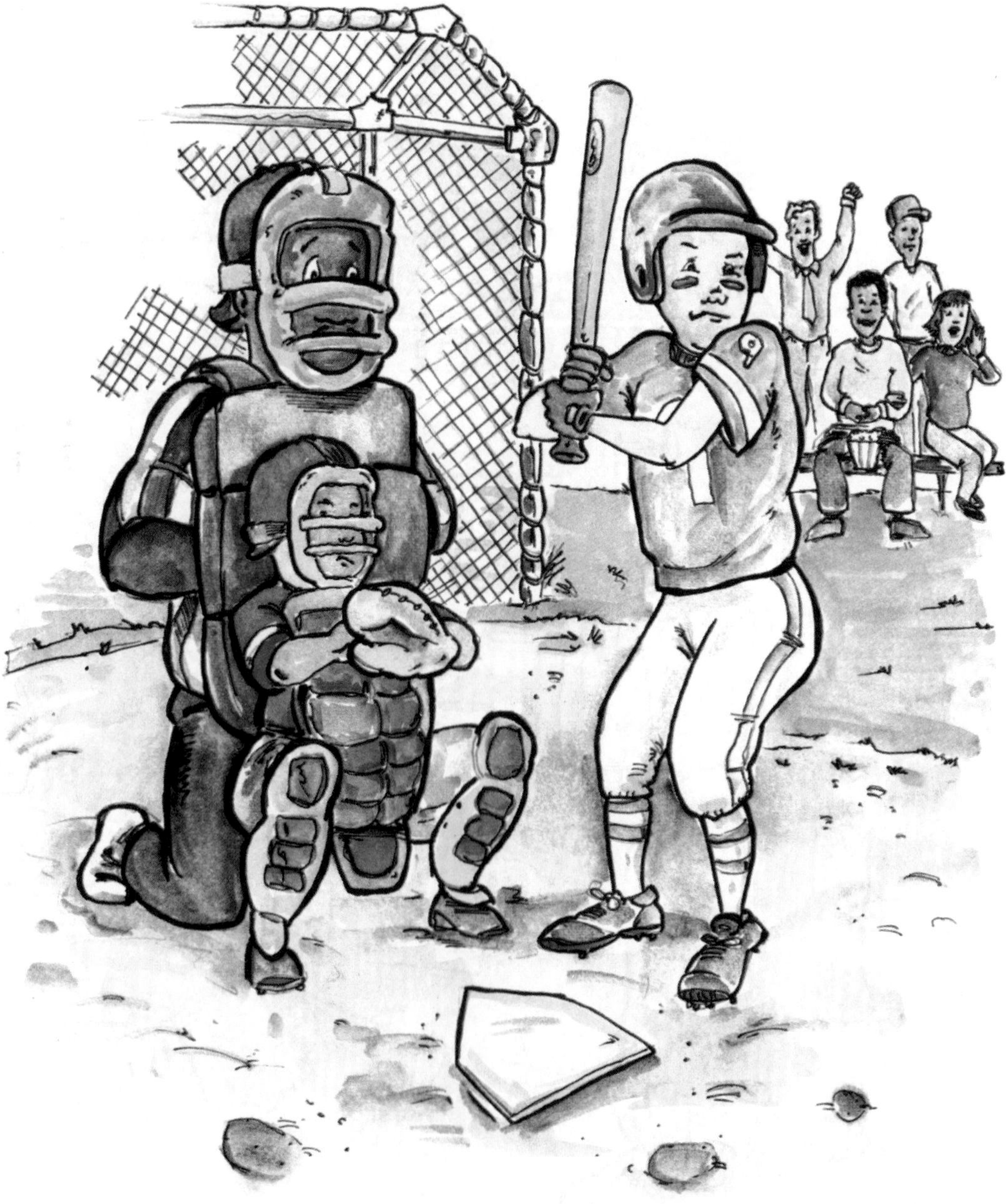

Principals play sports.

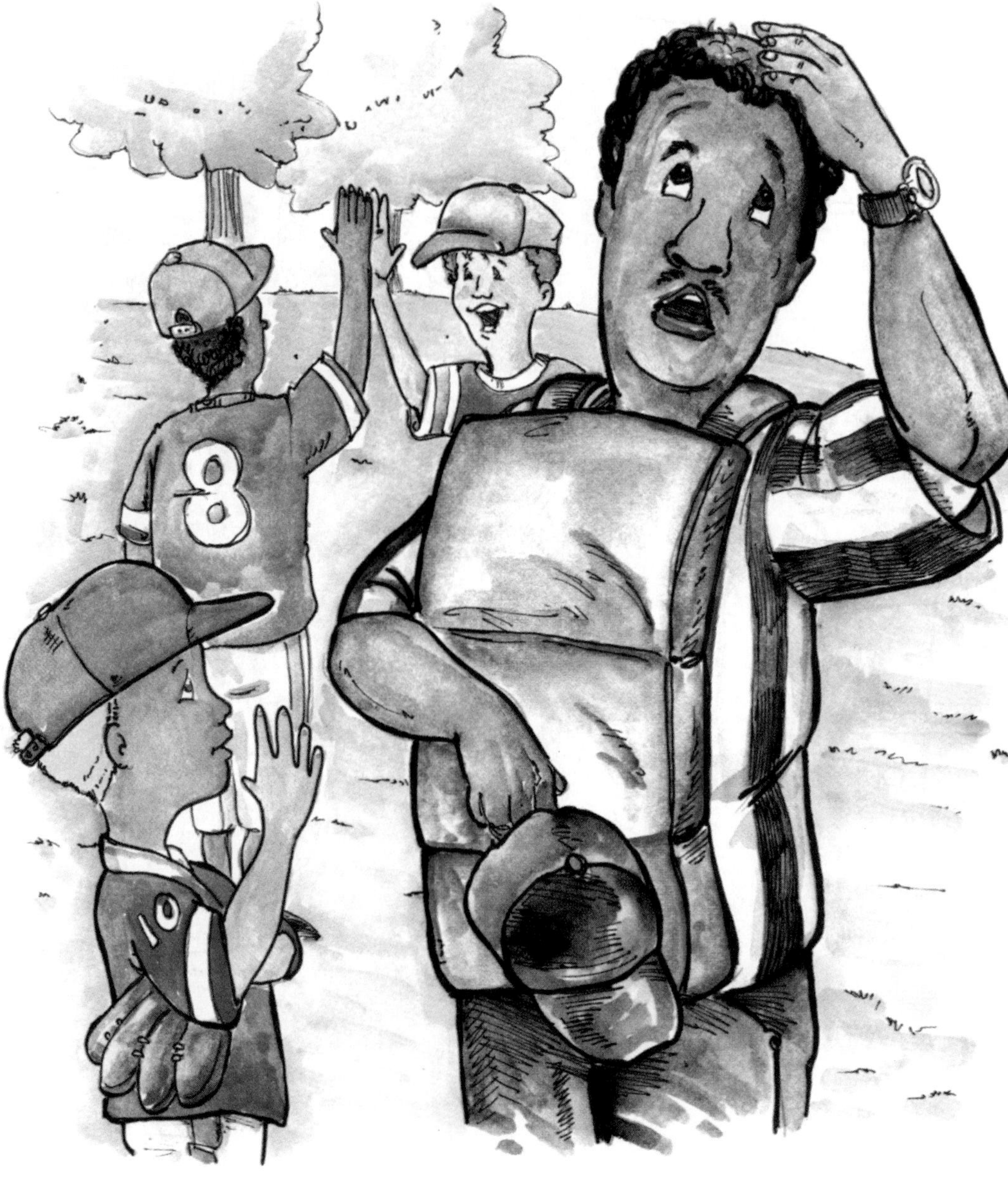

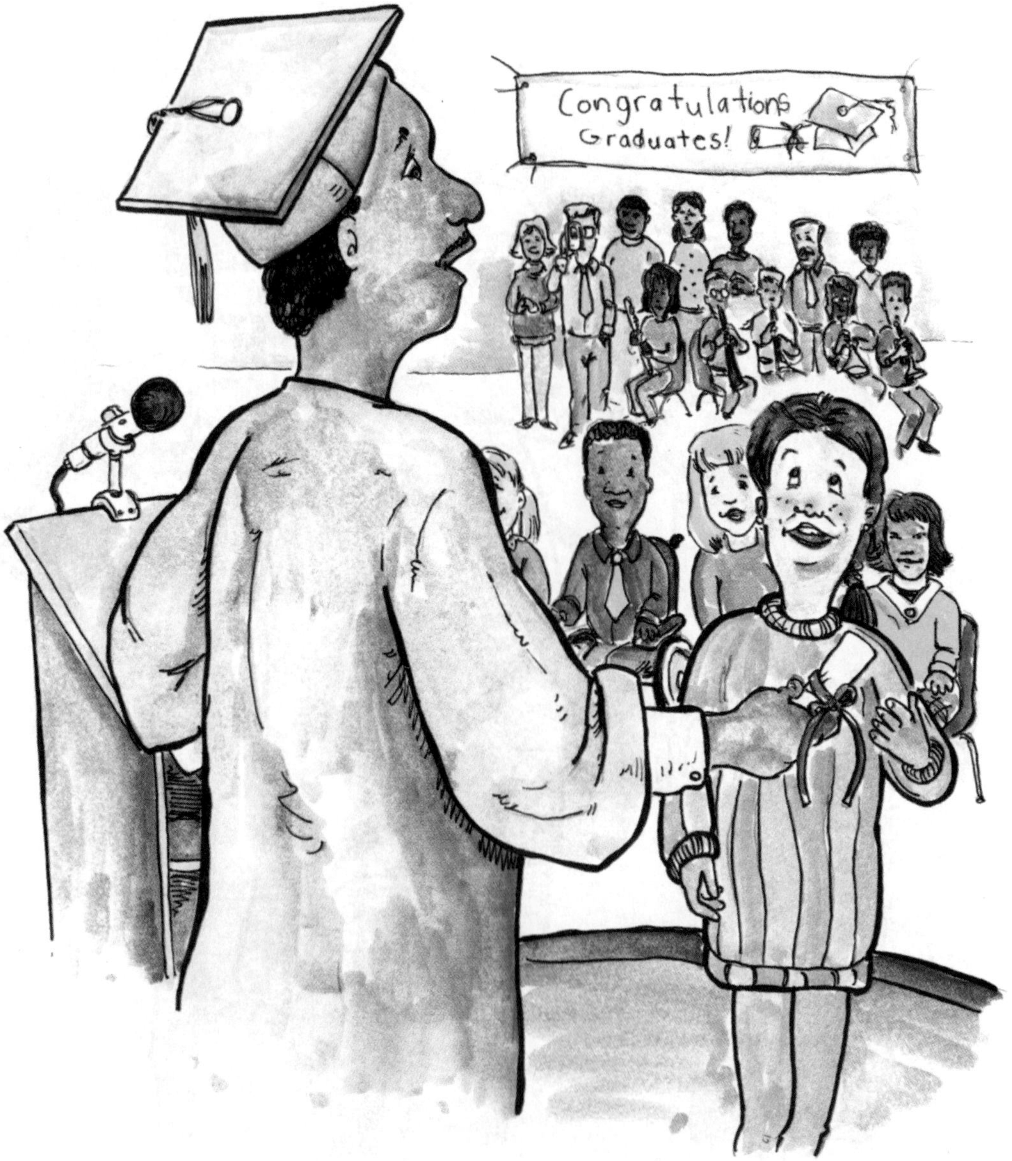
Congratulations
Graduates!

Principals dress up.

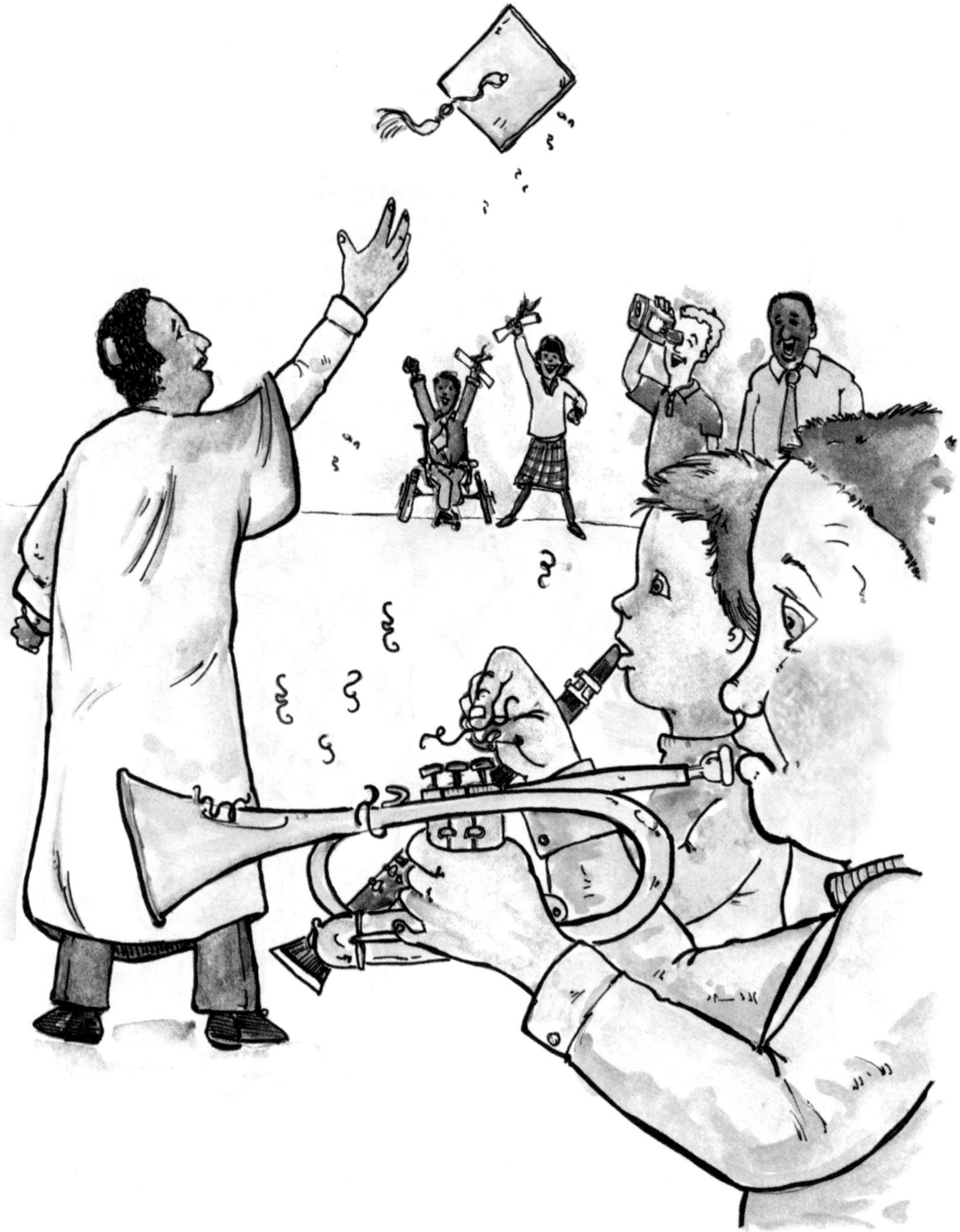

Principals take day trips.

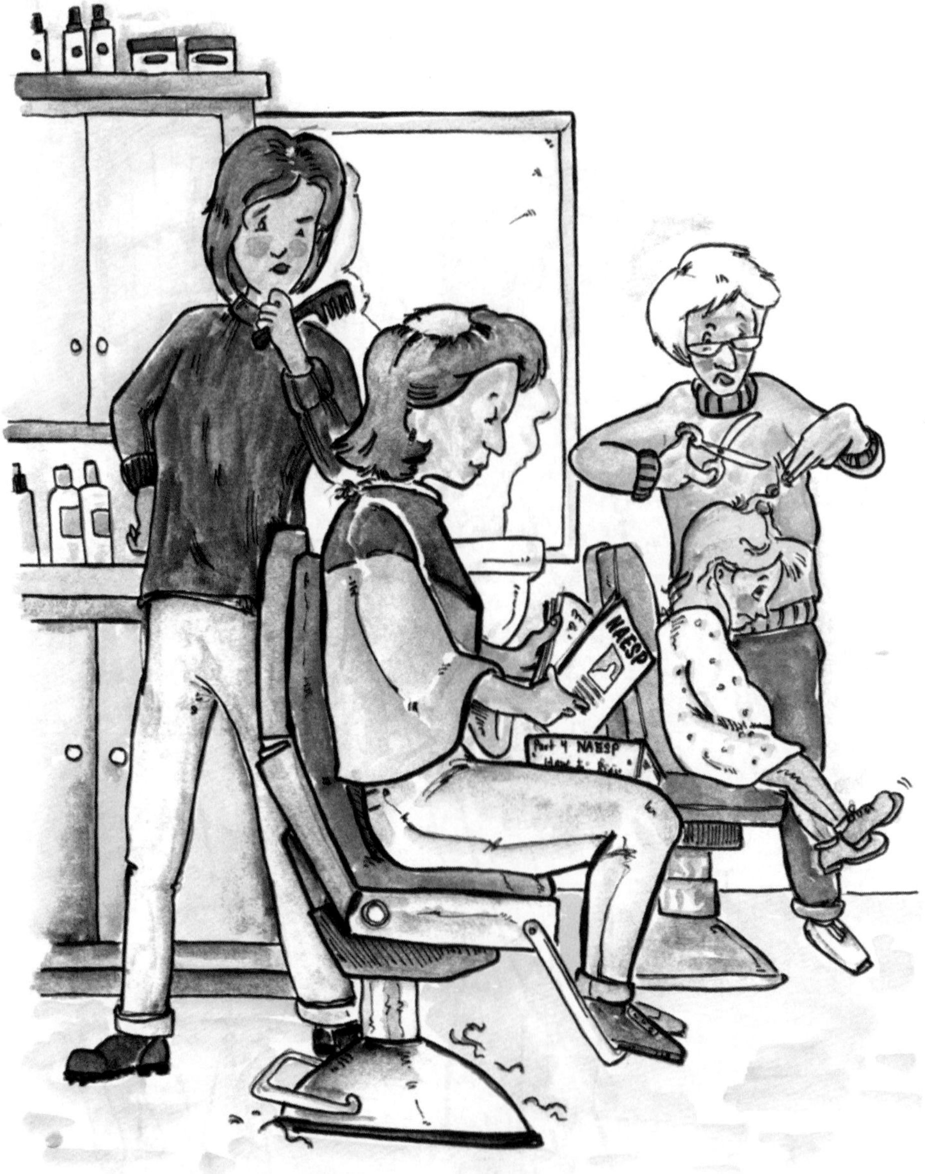
NAESP
Part 4 NAESP

Principals . . .

NAESP
Part 2
How to

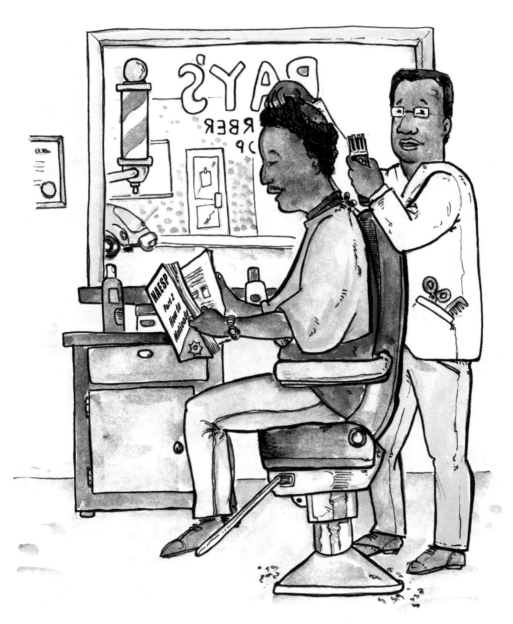

pamper themselves.

Principals . . .

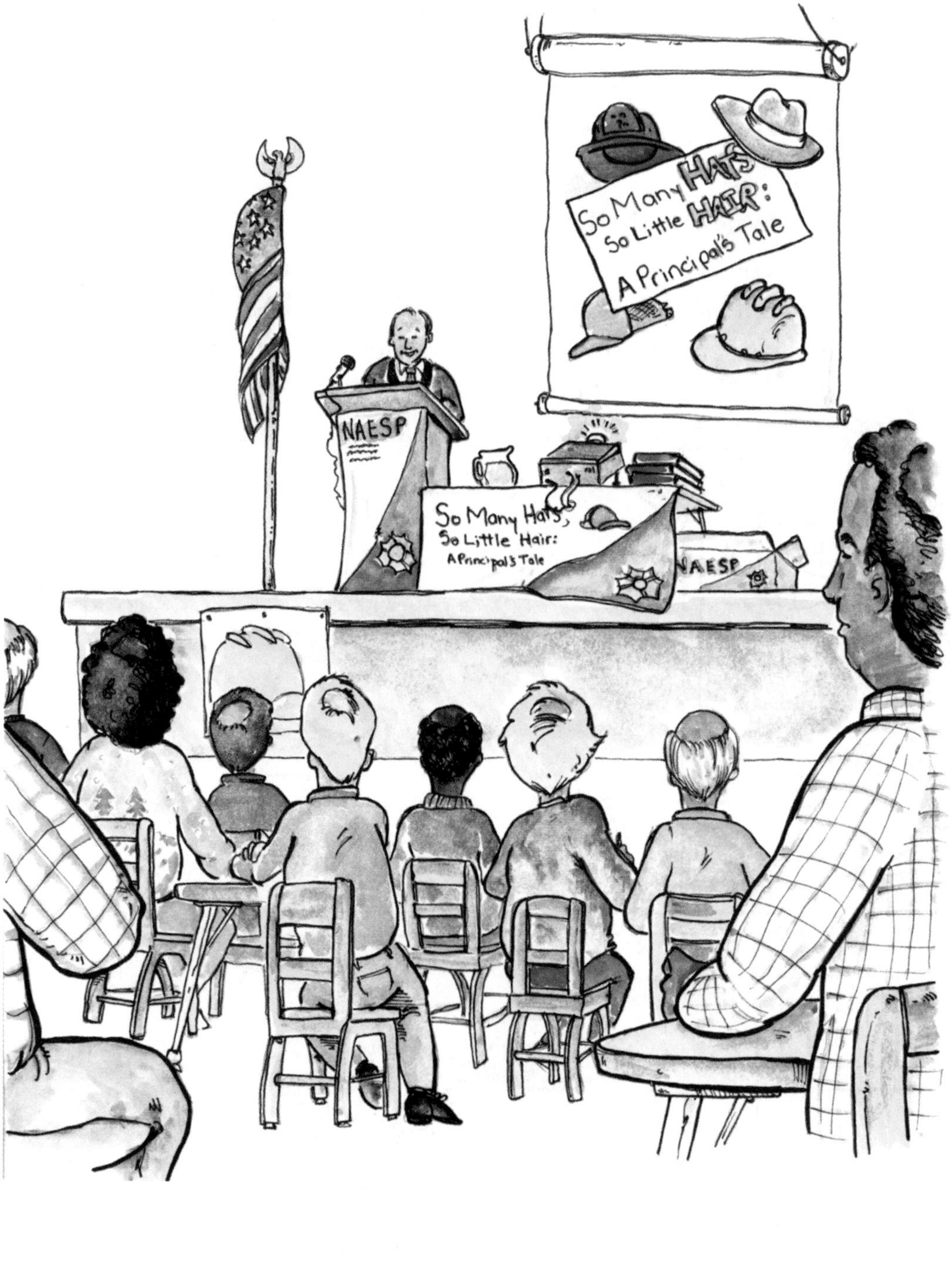
So Many HATS
So Little HAIR:
A Principal's Tale
NAESP
So Many Hats,
So Little Hair:
A Principal's Tale
NAESP

support one another.

All in a Day's Work: A Salute to Principals

With each career comes the highs and lows, the celebrations and frustrations one invariably accepts as normal and natural facts of life. So with equal parts informed realism and cautious optimism, Heather and Josh began their individual tenures as school principals. They knew the hallway ahead would be bumpy, and they agreed to support one another through thick and thin. They were out to make a difference.

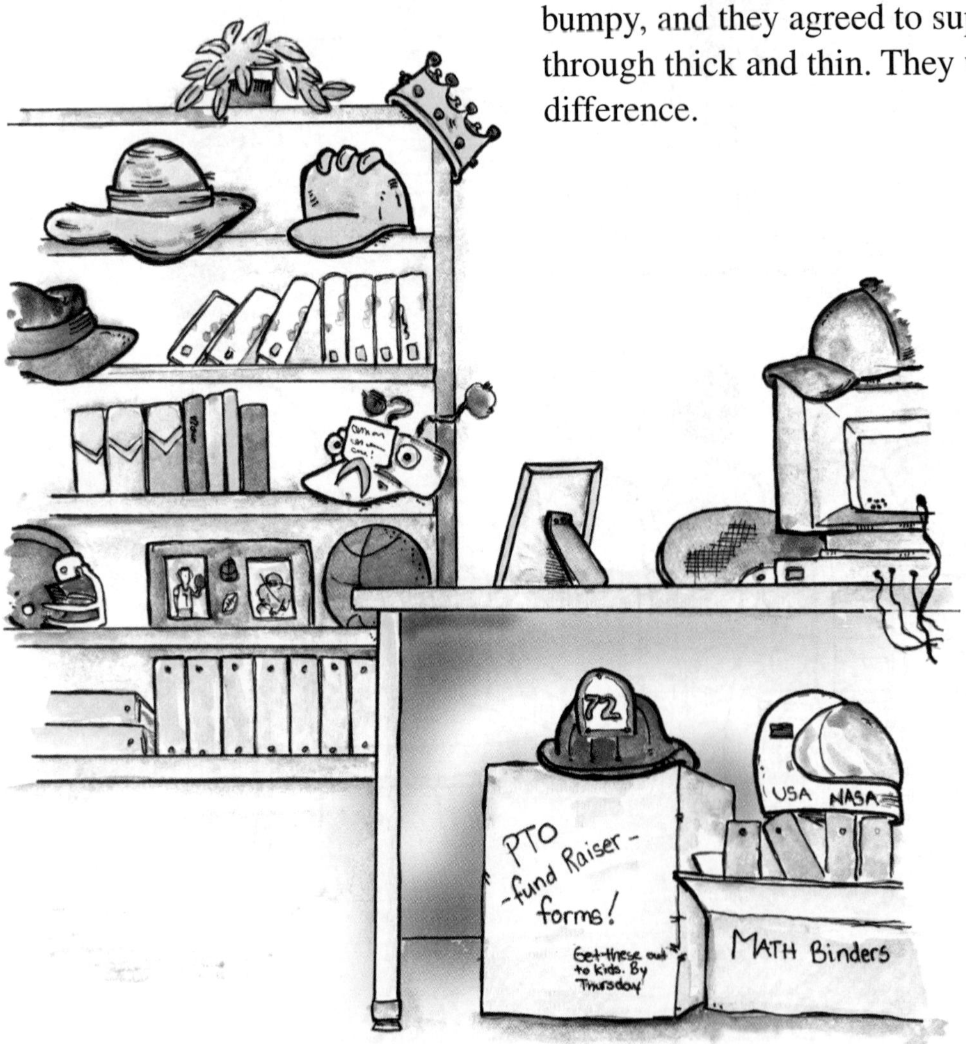
72
USA
NASA
PTO
-fund Raiser -
forms!
Get these out to kids. By Thursday
MATH Binders

When it came time for parent-teacher conferences, Heather was prepared to step in from time to time as guest mediator. And when the elementary school students asked Josh to be lead turkey in their annual holiday play, he accepted the role with good humor and grace. Heather could handle the early morning weather update calls from the town highway department. And Josh was more than happy to participate in community fund-raisers. Both were often the first to unlock the doors to their schools in the morning, and the last ones to turn out the lights at night.

As former classroom teachers these principals were inured to the growing responsibilities required of schools and educators. But with each passing day, discipline, student home-life, school-funding, and educational-requirement concerns demanded more and more of their individual attention. Some days they figuratively as well as literally changed hats so many times they gave new meaning to "hat head" and "thinning hair."

One spring Josh and Heather ran into one another at a national conference for principals. Before they even said "hello," Heather just smiled at Josh and said, "So many hats." Josh smiled back and responded, "So little hair." They now understood full well what Mrs. Allen's words, spoken many years before, really meant. They laughed, and joined the other principals who, like them, had gathered together to make a difference.